BASICS OF A
SUCCESSFUL
BUSINESS
STRATEGY

BASICS OF A SUCCESSFUL BUSINESS STRATEGY

KERSTIN FRIEDRICH AND LOTHAR J SEIWERT

KOGAN
PAGE

First published in 1992 in German entitled *Das 1x1 der Erfolgsstrategie* by Frankfurter Allgemeine Zeitung Informationsdienste and GABAL-Verlag

This edition, translated by Sally Lansdell Yeung, published in 1994

Kogan Page Limited
120 Pentonville Road
London N1 9JN

British Library Cataloguing in Publication Data

A CIP record for this book is available from the British Library.

ISBN 0-7494-1096-5

Printed and bound in Great Britain by
Biddles Limited, Guildford and King's Lynn

Contents

Foreword

Your success depends not on the extent of your intelligence, your knowledge or your resources, but purely and simply on your strategy, that is, the way in which you apply your energy and resources.

Since there are many different interpretations of strategy, nearly any form of planned action can be designated as strategic. Strategy in the context of the EKS strategy, however, means concentrating your energy on the crucial factors at an effective point.

For as long as you fail to keep your strategy on the right track, you will from year to year automatically waste more time and effort and be less secure and less successful. EKS is a system for the effective use of any kind of energy. Its principles are valid for a wide range of systems, whether biological, social or economic forces are involved.

Whether you want to improve the success of your firm or your department, your management of yourself or your career, you must mobilise your energy and concentrate it on the point of greatest impact. Successful business people and leaders have always – consciously or unconsciously – used a definite strategy. The EKS strategy which I developed shows you too the way to unrivalled peak performance.

The authors, Dr Kerstin Friedrich and Professor Dr Lothar J Seiwert, have both practised the EKS strategy extremely successfully over many years. In this book they have succeeded particularly well in describing the essential elements of the EKS strategy in a way which is clear and consistently well structured. It is also vivid and user friendly and the presentation is instructive and methodical. Their experience as seminar leaders and business consultants has stood them in good stead in this regard.

Humanity is not at the end of its capabilities, but only at the beginning. Not crisis management but opportunity management is what is required. To this end I wish you luck and a successful future with the EKS strategy.

Wolfgang Mewes, creator of EKS
Frankfurt, January 1994

Preface

Basics of a Successful Business Strategy introduces one of the most well-known and also most significant theories of success, Wolfgang Mewes' EKS strategy (cybernetic management theory).

Dr Kerstin Friedrich and Professor Dr Lothar J Seiwert deserve credit for having described in around 85 pages the most important elements of the EKS success strategy in a way that is graphic and informative and so helpful for both right-brain and left-brain thinking, while retaining all its inherent qualities. Anyone can in a short time – about 90 minutes – obtain an excellent introduction to the basic principles of EKS and each individual stage of putting it into practice.

The authors and publishers are convinced that *Basics of a Successful Business Strategy* offers its readers particular benefits and is another potential bestseller which will give many people advice about how they can increase their own success. We wish our new publication a wide circulation and our readers the best of success through reading it.

Why and how this programme was designed for you

Basics of a Successful Business Strategy has been prepared for you based on the latest theories of how we learn and how our brain functions. Each of the chapters is self-contained and follows the same design:

- The four success principles will each be outlined across a double page.
- The seven stages of the success strategy for peak performance and market leadership will each be described across two double pages using the same structure and appearance. The most important underlying arguments, know-how, actions, possible solutions and steps towards change will be represented clearly and practically by asking four questions – Why? How? Which? What?

Theoretical foundation		Practical translation	
Why is this stage important for your success strategy? • Description of the underlying arguments, benefits and significance of each chapter or stage for the reader.	*How* can you put this stage into practice? • Guidance on actions and possible solutions in the form of key points.	*Which* questions will enable you to make concrete progress (brainwriting)? • For each of the 7 stages there is a checklist of questions to work through and room to make notes.	*What* are the next steps towards change? • For each of the 7 stages of the success strategy there are 4 to 6 suggestions with space to record your progress.

This programme is aimed at two target groups:

- Entrepreneurs, directors, managers or supervisors who want to achieve better strategic planning, decision-making and action in their organisation.
- Individuals whose strategy is to improve their career prospects either inside or outside their organisation by achieving peak performance.

Strategic thinking and action

The strategy of the most successful organisations

Haven't you often asked yourself why some organisations are always a long way ahead of others? And this is true even when competition is becoming still more fierce and unpredictable. Is it chance, luck, talent or an above-average willingness to take risks?

These questions also troubled business researcher Wolfgang Mewes. He analysed the outstanding success stories of more than a thousand managers and organisations. He discovered that they all – whether consciously or unconsciously – followed a similar strategy. Mewes' conclusion was that *success is purely and simply a question of the right strategy!*

Strategy can be learnt

You can find the way to unrivalled peak performance

In the 1970s, Mewes succeeded in bringing together the common features of the greatest organisational and career success stories into a methodology which was published as a distance-learning course. This made it possible for anyone to learn how to think and act strategically. Strategic thinking is a 'key technology': it determines how, and how successfully, you can apply your energy and resources.

EKS users

Who can become successful with the EKS strategy?

The EKS strategy opens up new perspectives for any organisation – whether it is a service organisation, a trading company or an industrial corporation – and equally whether it has two, two hundred or two thousand employees. You can also use the EKS strategy if you are an employee, freelance or academic – you still operate in an environment where people are working with and for each other. Countless EKS users have shown that even with limited resources you can become a market leader – it is merely a question of how and on what you focus your effort. As everybody knows, even a hornet can put an elephant out of action – if it uses its efforts in the right way.

Why do you need a strategy?

Our performance-oriented society is in a state of continual change – indeed, change is the only constant. High-speed management, lean production, total quality management, just-in-time and other trends represent new challenges for organisations and managers. No longer do big organisations dominate small ones, but instead the fast overtake the slow. Ultimately, it is the one with the best strategy which will be successful.

'A strategy of focusing on obstacles leads to unrivalled peak performance'

You need a new success strategy	Very true	Partly true	Not true
1. If your organisation is facing stiff competition and your sales are not growing.			
2. If you want to improve or secure your market position.			
3. If you are looking for new business areas or distribution channels.			
4. If you are dependent on only a few customers or suppliers.			
5. If you want to set up a business with the lowest possible risk.			
6. If you have to restructure your organisation.			
7. If you want to get ahead in your career.			
8. If you want to be known as the best problem-solver in your organisation.			
9. If you want to become a sought-after specialist in the job market.			
10. Or if you quite simply want to be more successful with less effort.			

Score 1 for each 'very true' and 0.5 for each 'partly true'.

Total:

If your score is 2.5 or more, the next 11 chapters, with the four basic principles and the seven stages of the EKS strategy, will show you how you can successfully hold your ground against the competition and achieve unrivalled peak performance. Each chapter contains easy-to-follow advice and practical tips.

How far do you think and act strategically?

Strategic self-assessment	Almost always	It depends	Almost never
1. To what extent do you work to clearly defined business objectives?			
2. Do you know how to react to changes in the environment in keeping with these changes?			
3. Do you take your relative strengths and potential for success into consideration in the way you approach the market?			
4. When you are gathering information, do you know enough about what is really strategically important for you?			
5. Do you direct your activities towards a clearly defined target group that you always bear in mind?			
6. How deeply do you think about better solutions to the problems of your target group?			
7. Do you consistently translate new ideas into action, instead of giving up or forgetting them?			
8. When you have to make a decision, do you have sound criteria against which to work?			
9. Are you able to identify among your daily tasks those that are important in the medium and long term?			
10. Do you regularly set aside time for strategic planning and for considering your overall business policy?			
Total the number of crosses:			
Multiply the result:	× 3 =	× 2 =	× 1 =

- **Add together the totals to give your personal strategy rating**

If your strategy rating is:	
Between 10 and 15 points	**Interpretation:** In general you operate without any strategic time or success management and do not get any further than organising yourself and your day. The step-by-step strategy for success can help you to improve the way you set your strategic priorities and focus your efforts.
Between 16 and 22 points	You try to pursue strategic time and success management; you just need to be a little more systematic and consistent to achieve a real breakthrough. The step-by-step strategy for success will help you to develop your personal success strategy and to plan practical actions and first steps towards change.
Between 23 and 30 points	Your strategic time and success management can already be described as good. You focus consistently on what is important. Keep it up! The step-by-step strategy for success will help you to achieve even more and ensure lasting success.

What are the next steps?

There are always several possibilities:

'If not now – when?'

1. You leaf through this book and realise how important a good strategy is – and you do nothing else! Very well: stay where you are – and make progress more or less by chance. You will at least know why this is the case.

2. You work through this book and begin to apply the EKS strategy consistently. Good luck – keep it up!

3. EKS is easy and difficult at the same time. Most people are able to define their target group and its most pressing problem relatively quickly, and soon everything becomes automatic. Some need several attempts before they have finally found the point of greatest impact and enter into their own spiral of success. These very failures are an important part of the learning process and consequently part of the EKS strategy.

4. If you want to plunge into or test your strategy concept – now, when your path to success is right in front of you – we recommend the comprehensive EKS course by Wolfgang Mewes.

Follow-up

We wish you luck and success on your personal journey, as well as the courage to stand out from the crowd in your own market niche.

For simplicity and clarity in this book we will use business terminology. If you want to use EKS as an individual you can substitute your own terms for such words as 'customers' or 'field of business': 'customers' could be your bosses, for example, and 'field of business' could correspond to your functional department ('professional field').

Kerstin Friedrich
Lothar J Seiwert

What is certain to make you more successful?

Through specialisation to peak performance

Only a specialist who uses his or her resources to the full can achieve peak performance. This is the most important requirement for a successful strategy – focus your energies and specialise in:

- what you know best, and
- what offers most benefits to your customers.

Instead of a wide, diversified offering you must focus on a market niche in which you can be number one. This stands on its head the view of many companies who set out to diversify to 'minimise the risk'. But diversification, as you will see, is ultimately only a waste of effort. And because of this waste of effort the business risk is not minimised but increased.

Don't diversify

If you waste your effort you will remain merely average

Failures and competitive pressures mainly result from a decisive error in strategy: a waste of effort. If you offer a whole range of products in several markets, you can at best only be average. The more you waste your effort, the more difficult it becomes to produce something really special. And something really special is what you must offer today in order to be more attractive than your competitors.

Practice makes perfect

If you specialise and focus on a definite task, you will automatically learn faster through constant repetition and further development of your problem-solving ability. This process can be observed particularly well in sport: first, top athletes always specialise in one discipline and, second, they only get to the top by regular training and repetition.

Why you will become market leader

You can only become market leader by specialising

Focusing your efforts and specialising produce a whole range of positive results: greater efficiency, better productivity and growing sales. This allows price reductions, which lead to greater demand and then higher profits. And you will achieve an ever stronger position in the market and with it more power.

'You cannot run with the hare and hunt with the hounds' (Proverb)

Being number one has many advantages

Market leader

- The market leader has the best conceivable position in the market: in a very small niche market it can be disproportionately more successful and secure than an average competitor in a large market.
- The market leader is well known and has credibility. It is assumed to be the most competent; it is the trend setter and has the smallest innovation risk. The market leader enjoys not only financial but also psychological and emotional advantages. The charisma of the number one is substantially greater than that of an average company – a phenomenon which could be said to be a law of nature.

Why the specialist must be successful

The enormous advantages that are available to the specialist who has succeeded in becoming number one in the market are relatively easy to explain: the more complex the market and the products or services within it, the more customers, business partners, staff and investors look for a main point of reference – and that is the market leader.

Orders, information, ideas, staff, capital, supplier discounts, offers of collaboration, even the support of the media and the authorities flow to the market leader in preference to a less well-known competitor. The rules of sport apply here too: the winner enjoys recognition, popularity and the favour of the media and sponsors, whereas the one who comes second is hardly even noticed – even when he or she is beaten by only a hundredth of a second.

What should you concentrate your strategy on to be most successful?

'Markets operate as
networks with all the
associated rules'

Think network instead of linear!

Like biological organisms, markets are networks. That means that a change in one element will lead inevitably to a change in the others – the whole system is always affected.

For example, giving your staff a pay rise causes a chain reaction: it immediately affects costs and profits and may lead to an increase in sales, but it can also have a demotivating effect on other staff and so has negative as well as positive consequences. In the same way, any business decision always has effects at different physical and psychological levels.

Use the rules of the market!

The relationships within a market or an organisation are like an enormous invisible net. If you are unlucky, you can become hopelessly tangled up in them and unable to act. However, if you recognise these links and the points of greatest impact within them, you can make use of them to reach your objectives.

Although we live and work in networks, most people still think and act as if what they do only has a limited effect: engineers improve technical processes, accountants only look at the financial aspects, etc. If you devote yourself to isolated problems, you are wasting your effort. On the other hand, if you concentrate on the core problem you will reach the best result with a low expenditure of resources.

How can you solve problems more or less automatically?

David against Goliath – a good example of a direct hit

The legend of David and Goliath illustrates that it is not the amount of resources used but the precise way they are used that is decisive for success. The story goes that the slim shepherd David defeated the much more powerful giant Goliath. How?

He won because he behaved in exactly the opposite way to his opponent, who struck out at him blindly. First, David focused his energy by using a stone and a sling and thereby increased his effectiveness. Second, he hit exactly the most effective point, namely the forehead.

The explanation is simple: the human body is a network and David found the node which controls the vital bodily functions. Nevertheless, you should not use the points of greatest impact in a system to knock out your competitors but to offer your customers the greatest possible benefits.

Not how but where you hit is decisive

In a network it is not a question of using the greatest possible amount of resources but of concentrating the available resources on the point of greatest impact in each case. In a network, if you find the central node for solving your particular problem, a chain reaction results.

The problems associated with the core problem automatically become easier to solve. The denser the network becomes – and this happens all the time in all markets – then the more important it is to target the point of greatest impact, otherwise you will have to try harder and harder and waste more and more energy.

'Give me but one firm spot on which to stand, and I will move the Earth' (Archimedes)

Point of greatest impact

19

How do you find the point of greatest impact?

'The target group will
enthusiastically demand
what it needs for its
development'

The art of management

The point of greatest impact is rarely as clearly visible in practice as in the well-known example of David and Goliath. Who is able to predict in today's ever more complex world which alternative will use resources most efficiently?

The art of management lies in identifying among the multitude of problems the core problem which is connected to all the others. When this problem is solved, solving the rest becomes much easier – they even sometimes solve themselves.

Plant growth

The point of greatest impact: nature shows the way

Natural scientist Justus von Liebig discovered 140 years ago how the point of greatest impact in a network could be identified when he was researching the cause of plant growth. He established that a plant needs four elements for growth. If any one element is lacking, the plant will not grow any further – even if all the other factors are available in abundance.

The art therefore consists in always supplying a system – or as appropriate for your target group or your customers – at the bottleneck, that is, what it currently most urgently needs for its development. Whoever is in a position to do this will immediately be in the strongest situation in the market.

So you achieve the greatest effect with minimal effort

Liebig's 'minimum' principle works as well in any business: whichever company offers its target group what it urgently needs for its further development has identified the point of greatest impact and possesses the key to success. The point which promises most efficient use of resources thus always centres on the obstacle to development. Whoever helps to overcome this obstacle can be sure of the greatest demand and the greatest success.

What has all this to do with you?

The internal minimum factor – obstacle to your own success

The EKS strategy uses the link which Liebig discovered between obstacles and growth in two ways:

'By removing the obstacle or minimum factor you can become the market leader'

- The internal minimum factor shows you your operational bottleneck, that is, the problem that is preventing your organisation from growing.
- If you concentrate all your resources on removing this bottleneck, your organisation will develop well.

The external minimum factor – the key to success

The external minimum factor limits the development and the success of your target group. If you are successful in making this minimum factor available to your target group, you have the best conditions for success.

Minimum factor

Whoever solves the target group's most pressing problem can be sure that this achievement will be sought out, accepted and paid for by the target group.

Set the right priorities!

The most important task, first of all, is to determine not your own minimum factor but that of your target group. Always think outwards and don't get too involved in your internal (eg, operational) problems. The more successfully you solve the problems of your target group, the more successfully you will also solve your own problems.

How do you find your optimum business objective?

The right objective decides your success

In any business every day there are countless decisions. The alternative you choose in each case will be decided according to your objectives: these lay down what you consider important or unimportant, what you aspire to or object to, what you take notice of or ignore. The better an organisation's objective-setting process, the better its flow of information, its decisions and its development as a whole.

Focus on benefits

Why profit maximisation is not a sensible objective in the long run

The objective of a business is to make the highest possible profit – at least that is the view of many theorists and practitioners today. Wolfgang Mewes found, however, that enduringly successful businesses always do their utmost to offer the greatest benefits to their customers. They thus put benefit maximisation before profit maximisation. Profits are still the inevitable result of benefit maximisation, but not the company's principal objective.

Profits serve the general good – or do they?

The direct pursuit of profit contradicts all natural laws. In evolution egotists – and there are no better profit maximisers – become extinct. But where would our society be today if there were no profits for investment, jobs or tax revenue? Thus without profits there would be no social benefits.

Does this mean that profit maximisation is nevertheless more important than benefit maximisation? Both are important – but cause and effect are reversed: the more you focus on benefits to society, the more your profits increase. As benefits are increased so interest and demand grow and thus automatically do turnover and the number of products sold. This benefit-focused strategy is 'indirect profit maximisation'.

22

How can you make money without maximising profits?

Small difference – big effect

The difference between direct and indirect, ie, benefit-focused, profit maximisation might at first glance appear to be negligible, but it is strategically decisive. This becomes obvious if you consider the different methods by which the two objectives can be reached:

- Direct profit maximisation can only be achieved through, at worst, deception and robbery, or through aggressive selling and the exercise of power.
- On the other hand, there is only one way to indirect profit maximisation, namely increasing benefits to society – still better for your tightly defined target group.

Particularly successful business people have shown us how to do this, such as Henry Ford.

Become the best benefit provider for your target group in seven steps!

The EKS strategy will help you to reach a position where you can increase the benefits to your target group and, as an indirect result, your profits. Wolfgang Mewes has described precisely how this works in his seven-stage concept:

1. Analysis of strengths.
2. Search for the most suitable business or professional field.
3. Selection of the most promising target group.
4. Analysis of problems within the target group.
5. Necessary innovation.
6. Skilful collaboration.
7. Specialisation in fulfilling a constant basic need.

This seven-stage concept is applicable to any situation and to any person – and equally so whether you want to further the success of your business or your own career.

'Solving other people's problems will make the most profit'

23

The strategy for success

A summary of the four basic principles of EKS is shown in the following diagram.

- **Principle 1**   Focus instead of wasted effort
- **Principle 2**   The point of greatest impact
- **Principle 3**   Minimum factor: bottleneck
- **Principle 4**   Benefit maximisation

How are the seven stages linked?

The seven-stage programme for market leadership and peak performance

The diagram shows how the individual stages of EKS relate to each other.

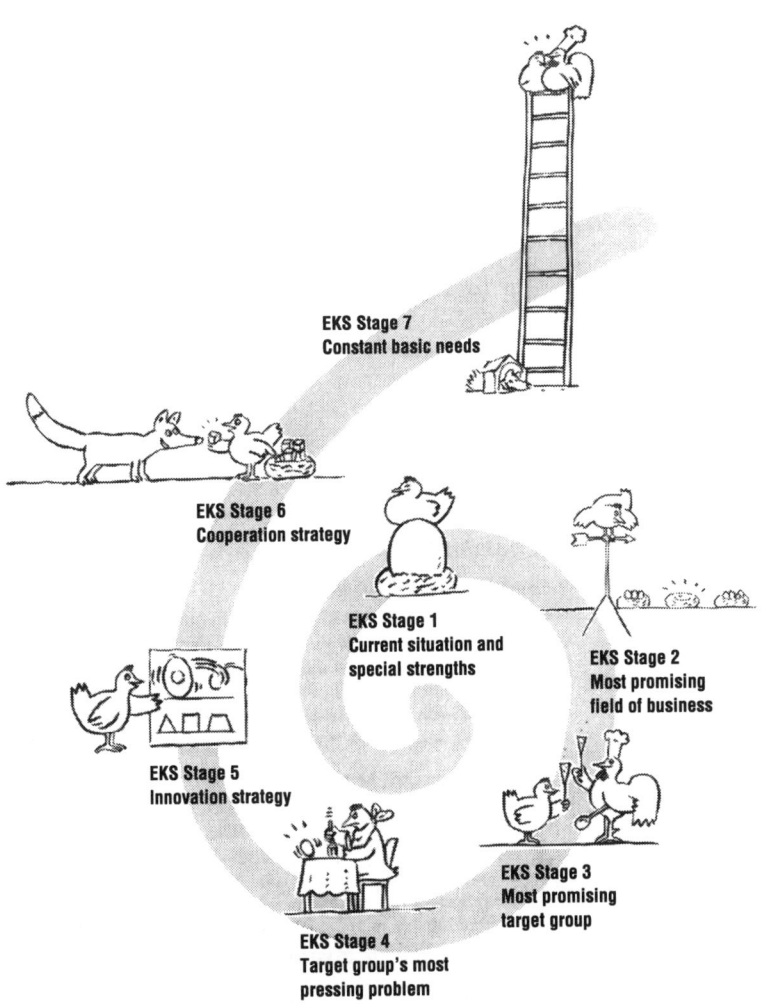

EKS Stage 7
Constant basic needs

EKS Stage 6
Cooperation strategy

EKS Stage 1
Current situation and
special strengths

EKS Stage 2
Most promising
field of business

EKS Stage 5
Innovation strategy

EKS Stage 3
Most promising
target group

EKS Stage 4
Target group's most
pressing problem

25

Why should you be aware of your special strengths?

'If you focus on your strengths, you can initially disregard your weaknesses'

1. Prerequisite for success: be different from the rest

Every organisation – including yours – has special strengths which distinguish it from its competitors: the combination of abilities, image and know-how that is as unique as a fingerprint. There is also a particular field of business for each organisation that suits its strengths and in which it is superior to all its competitors. You must above all else identify your special strengths and work out clearly what they are. Unfortunately, many managers try to copy supposedly superior competitors. It is better to create a distinct profile for yourself so that you will be different from the rest.

Strengths profile

2. Develop strengths – disregard weaknesses

Improvement in the context of the EKS strategy means developing your strengths. Many people think that they have to combat their weaknesses to be successful. They focus on learning and improving all kinds of things. This is futile, however, for two reasons:

- First, you will only be average if you neglect your strengths in favour of your weaknesses.
- Second, you will inevitably be demotivated if you are preoccupied with your weaknesses.

Competence

3. Acquire visible competence

If you only know approximately where your special strengths lie, you will merely be able to convey them approximately to your target group. Only if you develop your strengths can they be revealed to the outside world in a distinct performance profile. This is necessary if you are to stand out from the crowd of competitors – and you will automatically increase your power of attraction.

4. Without the present there is no future

If you want to improve something you must know where you are starting from. People often restrict themselves to analysing financial accounts, sales figures and costs. Other things are responsible for lasting success, such as intangible factors like know-how, image or customer loyalty. These will be systematically covered in the first step.

How do you find your special strengths?

A comprehensive analysis of the current situation covers four areas:

'There is a market for what every person and every organisation produces'

1. Work out what you have done up to now – and what else you could have done

Make a list of all your organisation's outputs and products. Consider what else could currently be produced. Ensure you include the intangible assets such as patents, licences and know-how. Be as thorough as possible about this. Average overall results can often mask potentially high-performing products.

2. Analyse the problems you have already solved

Experience

Which problems have already been handled successfully in your organisation? Work out which problems you have solved or could solve better than other companies. Determine which problems you have yourself which require a change to occur, and which customer problems you are aware of. No problem is unique –many other people are certain to have the same problem. When you have done this exercise you have made the first step towards discovering a market niche.

3. Describe your vision and goals

Vision

Every person, including every manager, has goals, dreams, ideals, models and visions. These also steer – consciously or unconsciously – the development of the organisation in a positive or negative direction. If you want to be number one at chess, you will behave differently from someone who wants to be at the top in tennis.

4. Investigate the relationships and image you have in the market

Relationships, image and other intangible assets are undervalued by people who are overwhelmingly materialistic. You can often see yourself better through someone else's eyes than through your own. Ask your colleagues, friends, customers and other business partners what opinion they have of you and what kind of image you project.

Which questions will enable you to make concrete progress?

Write down the first words
and thoughts that come
into your head

1. Abilities and achievements

- Which products or services does your organisation provide, and which products or services could it provide?
- How is what you offer distinguished from the competition (quality, price, service, etc)?
- In which area is your market share greatest?
- What would you like to do most, and what would your organisation be most suited to?

2. Problem-solving experience

- Which target group problems has your organisation solved up to now?
- Which internal problems have been solved up to now?
- Which customer problems could still be solved?

3. Visions and goals

- What dreams and visions do you have for your organisation?
- What is your business philosophy?
- What are your business objectives?

4. Relationships and image

- With which target groups does your organisation have a particularly good relationship?
- What do your customers think you are best at?
- Which useful relationships do you have (customers, business partners, media, politicians etc)?

What are the next steps towards your special strengths?

1. Write down strengths at random and select intuitively

Note down all the strengths that you identified in answer to the questions on page 28, without imposing any order or value on them. Then mark those that seem to you intuitively to be the most important.

Absolute strengths

2. Determine relative strengths compared to the competition

Now ask yourself how strong these attributes are in relation to a typical competitor (rate on a scale of 0 to 100, see the bottom of this page).

Relative strengths

3. Assess strengths in the eyes of the target group

Now ask yourself how your target group would rate these strengths. Deviations from your own rating will give you pointers to whether your picture of yourself differs from the one outsiders have of you. Think about the causes!

Target group

4. Work out greatest, most promising strengths

Sort out the highest-rated strengths and transfer them with their accompanying scores to the box at the end of this page. Now contemplate your strengths profile! Which are the most obvious strengths? Does a combination of individual strengths already result in outstanding performance?

Greatest strengths

5. Assess the degree of personal identification

Can you identify with the result? If not, look for other combinations. You will only do well if you like what you are doing – and that must be the result of your strategy.

Combining strengths

6. The strengths profile of my organisation:	0 50 100
•	
•	
•	

Scale: 0 = well below average in comparison with the competition; 50 = average in comparison with the competition; 100 = well above average in comparison with the competition.

Why do strengths and field of business go together?

'I would rather be first in a village than second at Rome' (Caesar)

1. Your strengths must fit your field of business like a key in a lock

The starting point of the second stage is the strengths profile. It is like a key for which the only suitable lock has to be found, ie, a suitable field of business. The field of business determined in Stage 2 is only intended as a preliminary rough guide. A final decision will not yet be made.

Market focus

2. Your greatest strength is worth nothing if no one is prepared to pay for it

Stage 2 is concerned with finding a field of business, that is a market, in which you can bring your strengths to bear in the best way. So now you should consider the possible applications of your special strengths.

Self-motivation

3. What you do well and like doing has the best chance of leading to peak performance

In the field of business that corresponds most closely to your own strengths, you can operate from the beginning with the greatest security and success. It is important that you can identify fully with your field of business.

4. You must decide on your field of business yourself and not be dictated to by others

Many managers and business people allow their field of business to be determined by outsiders – either by customers, whom you always want to please, or by competitors, who seem to control a large part of the market.

5. It is better to be first in a small field of business than to be average in a large one

It is important to look from the start for a field of business that is precisely related to your own resources. To begin with it is better to choose one that is too small than one that is too large.

30

How do you find your most promising field of business?

1. Extract from your strengths profile as many fields of business as possible

You can often take the field of business directly from the strengths profile. Nevertheless, don't give up the search too early but consider the possibilities deeply and methodically. While a certain amount of precision is necessary, you should not take this to extremes. To begin with a rough guide is sufficient.

'Do it, try it, fix it'
(Peters and Waterman)

2. The more narrowly you define your field of business, the faster your market share will grow

The more precisely you can define your field of business, the faster you will experience your first successes, the stronger your motivation will be and the faster your rate of growth. Quick initial successes are important: they encourage a chain reaction of other positive effects.

Narrow field of business

3. You can expand your field of business if you remain true to your strengths

Don't worry about defining a field of business that is too small to begin with! When you have achieved some initial success and thus opened up the market niche, you will be able progressively to expand your field of business.

4. Always remember: 'test the theory'

Don't turn your potential fields of business over in your mind for days and months on end, but put them to the test as quickly as possible. The 'trial and error' method always takes precedence in the EKS strategy: you take a small step in a direction which is basically the right one and learn from the experience you gain. That is, you make any adjustments that are necessary and then test the next step in the same way. By doing this you keep the risks to a minimum.

Test fields of business

Which questions will enable you to make firm progress?

**Write down the first words
and thoughts that come
into your head**

1. Which fields of business result directly from your special strengths?

2. Which other applications and market openings do you see for your strengths?

3. Which fields of business result from combining individual strengths?

4. Which problems could be solved by your special strengths?

5. Which business and professional fields has your organisation been involved in up to now?

6. Which business and professional fields is your organisation involved in at present?

7. In which fields of business has your organisation had the strongest market position up to now?

8. In which fields of business could your organisation become market leader relatively quickly?

9. Which fields of business do you identify with most strongly?

10. In which field of business is demand greatest?

What are the next steps towards the most promising field of business?

1. Make a list of as many fields of business as possible

Do this regardless of whether or not they can be attained at present. With the help of Stages 5 and 6 (innovation and collaboration strategies) you will be able to solve problems that at the moment seem insurmountable.

2. Use your intuition to look for some promising fields of business

Intuition

Include those that you have a strong inclination towards, that you think are attainable or where you already have a strong market position.

3. Evaluate your fields of business

Evaluation

- Which fields of business are most in tune with your special strengths (key fits lock!)?
- Which fields of business would you most prefer to be active in?
- In which fields of business do you have the greatest potential for market leadership?

Promising fields of business:	Strengths	Priority	Potential	Total

- Enter scores between 0 and 100. 100 points = highest score, that is, complete correspondence with strengths or highest priority or highest market potential.
- Add the scores together horizontally and complete the 'total' column. The highest score gives you a pointer to the most promising field of business.

4. My most promising field of business is:

33

Summary: Seven principles for strategic strengths analysis

Stage 1: Current situation and strengths analysis

1. Be different from the rest – become unique.

2. Concentrate on developing your strengths – disregard your weaknesses.

3. Analyse your current situation – you will discover your special strengths.

4. Search continually for your strengths – they exist everywhere.

5. Identify your greatest strengths and combine them to give new products and services.

6. Develop your own unmistakeable strengths and performance profile.

7. Keep a sharp eye open for new areas of operation and opportunities.

Implementation

Be sure to relate this stage fully to your own personal or business circumstances. Capture briefly your three most important thoughts or insights. 'Don't only th-ink it, ink it!' A catch phrase or a representative key word is sufficient.

My three most important thoughts, insights, key words:
-
-
-

Summary: Seven principles for promising fields of business

Stage 2: Most promising field of business

1. Your strengths are your key, so make sure your field of business is a suitable lock.

2. It is better to be first in a small field of business than second somewhere else.

3. What you do well and like doing is alwo what makes you successful = peak performance.

4. The more narrowly you define your field of business, the more quickly you will see success.

5. Deploy your special strengths in the most promising field of business.

6. Through trial and error find the most suitable field of business for your strengths profile.

7. You can expand as much as you choose as long as you stay true to your strengths.

Be sure to relate this stage fully to your own personal or business circumstances. Capture briefly your three most important thoughts or insights. 'Don't only th-ink it, ink it!' A catch phrase or a representative key word is sufficient.

Implementation

My three most important thoughts, insights, key words:
-
-
-

35

Why concentrate on target groups instead of fields of business?

'The people are the market'

1. Your products and services are not intended for abstract fields of business but for people (= target group)

Therefore in the third stage of the EKS strategy look for the most promising target group within your field of business. Your products and services are not intended for an abstract market but always for people. A target group in the context of the EKS strategy is a group of people with the same desires, needs or problems.

Dialogue

2. Only through dialogue with your target group can you develop your products and services to unrivalled peak performance

You won't find your most promising target group by theoretical discussions around the boardroom table. And without feedback you will find it difficult to offer a custom-made product or service. Don't forget: what you offer must be adapted to the wishes of your target group – and not the other way round.

Learning process

3. Focusing yourself on your target group triggers a learning process

You recognise changes in the needs, problems and resistance of the target group more precisely and faster than the competition – and thereby secure yourself a lasting competitive advantage. By the same token, the target group gets to know your products and services better. Without this mutual learning process your organisation will develop rather by chance.

4. Only through segmenting your target group precisely can you find a suitable market niche

The more thoroughly you define your target group, the more clearly you can align your products or services to their special needs. The feedback from your target group will steer you automatically to the most promising market niche.

5. Your target group is more important than your capital assets

Your organisation's intangible assets, like competitive advantage, customer relationships or market power, will grow relatively quickly and raise with them your yield and market worth. Your strategic target is to become the leading provider of benefits for your target group!

How do you find your most promising target group?

1. Ascertain the target groups within your field of business

Proceed methodically as in Stages 1 and 2 by brainstorming. Look for as many target groups as possible. For example, within the business field 'cleaning' there are the problems of cleaning office blocks, factories, hospitals and so on. Each of these target groups can be segmented still further – according to their size, their regional distribution and many other criteria.

'Precise focus on a target group is the most important strategic success factor'

2. Find out which target group has the most urgent need for what you offer

Look for the target group whose problems correspond most closely with your problem-solving abilities. If you believe that you could solve problems equally well for different target groups, you must initially decide on one of these. You will only succeed in doing this through practical target group tests. Formulate your offering and take it to representatives of the target group. Record the negative reactions as carefully as the positive ones!

Needs analysis

3. Analyse your present customers: which are the most agreeable and most lucrative? Which are most in sympathy with you?

Ask these customers why they buy from you and not the competition. This analysis will again give you pointers to your special problem-solving abilities and to the most promising target group.

Customer analysis

4. Formulate your ideal target group

Ideals have a tendency to become reality. So ask yourself what the ideal target group for your product or service would look like. Then search systematically for people that actually have these characteristics. Try to define the target group in concrete terms, and find out which media can be used to reach them.

Which questions will enable you to make firm progress?

Write down the first words and thoughts that come into your head

1. Which target group corresponds to your organisation's strengths?

2. Which target groups did your organisation use to have?

3. Which target groups does your organisation have now?

4. Which target groups do you find most agreeable and profitable?

5. For which target groups do you solve a particularly pressing problem?

6. For which target groups could you solve a particularly pressing problem?

7. Which target group has or could have the most urgent need for what you offer?

8. Which target groups are most attracted to your organisation?

9. What would your favourite customer look like?

10. What does the target group look like that is theoretically best for your field of business?

What are the next steps towards the most promising target group?

1. Identify as many target groups as possible

Don't let it worry you if you have had no contact at all up to now with a particular customer group. There are many economical ways in which you can test whether these target groups react favourably to what you have to offer.

'The clearer and more homogeneous that target group, the easier their problems and priorities are recognised'

2. Use your intuition to look for a number of promising target groups

As a rule these will be those with whom you already have a good relationship or whose problems you think you would be best at solving.

Intuition

3. Evaluate your target groups according to the following criteria:

- Which target groups have the greatest need for your products or services?
- With which target groups do you have the best contact?
- To which target group can you offer the greatest benefits?

Evaluation

Promising target groups	*Need*	*Contact*	*Benefits*	**Total**

- Enter scores between 0 and 100. 100 points = highest score, ie, greatest need in the target group or best contact or greatest potential benefits.
- Add the scores together horizontally and complete the 'total' column. The highest score gives you a pointer to the most promising target group. *Caution*: you will not find the most promising target group through systematic evaluation, but only through practical tests! This preparatory work merely offers a rough guide.

4. My most promising target group is:

39

Why is the most pressing problem so significant for your success?

'Problems are opportunities in disguise'

1. Your organisation exists primarily in order to solve problems and only secondarily to sell products

An organisation's success is not decided by the size of its resources and reserves, but by its ability to focus its products and services on the most pressing problems of its target group in a better and more precise way than its competitors.

2. Everything you offer must solve a customer problem

The bigger the problem, the greater the acceptance and demand for a product or service that exactly solves it. Where vitally important problems are concerned, many people are prepared to clutch at any straw without hesitation.

Market opportunities

3. The more problems the better!

Behind every problem is the need for a solution. And every solution to a problem is immediately a market opportunity which promises turnover and profit. Many people are inclined to stay out of the way of problems. You should behave differently – use the opportunities that are hiding behind the problems.

4. The more precisely you aim at your target group's problem, the greater your success will be

Caution: the decisive factor is which problem the target group perceives to be the most important – and not the one that you think important. As soon as you have solved the problem which is currently perceived to be the most pressing, you must move on to the next. Only in this way can you attain long-term peak performance. The 'path of the most pressing problems' which emerges also shows you the way to risk-free specialisation. (For further details see Stage 7, 'The constant basic need'.)

40

How do you find your target group's most pressing problem?

Note: You can only discover the most pressing problem through direct contact with your target group. The following questions and evaluation grid will get you started on this stage.

> 'I can only really understand someone else when I have run several miles in his moccasins' (Indian saying)

1. Focus your thoughts outwards

You will only find your target group's most pressing problem if you centre your thinking on the question: 'How can I increase the benefits to my target group?' The more successfully you solve the problems of your target group, the better you will also solve your own. Demand, turnover and profits then increase automatically.

2. Put yourself in your target group's shoes and understand for yourself the problems they could have

Analysis of problems

Your most important focusing tool is a periodic analysis of needs and problems. This will allow you to be certain that you are always reacting to changing requirements – and that you discover new market opportunities before all other competitors. You could survey the target groups on an ongoing basis or at particular times. This will bring the target group's problems to light more reliably than supposition and speculation.

3. Run through in your mind the development, use and disposal of your products; consider the problems which could arise

Note down any problems you identify during this study. Discuss the result with representatives of your target group and find out which problems are the most urgent.

4. Define the most pressing problem through dialogue with your target group

Dialogue

Identify the most pressing problem, work out a proposed solution and discuss it with representatives of your target group with whom you have a good relationship. Different target groups have different, sometimes contradictory problems. This makes communication more difficult because the feedback can be confused and distorted. If this is the case the target group must be defined still more narrowly.

41

Which questions will enable you to make firm progress?

Write down the first words
and thoughts that come
into your head

1. Which target group problems, ie, which desires, needs, concerns and complaints, are you already aware of?

2. Which problems do you already solve and which could you find a better solution for?

3. Which customers have you lost in the past? Ask yourself why.

4. Which customers have you won recently – and why?

5. What are your customers' reactions to what you offer? Don't only think about the volume of orders, but also about emotional responses like sympathy or rejection.

6. What would your most pressing problem be if you were in your target group's situation?

7. Which problems could arise which are related to your organisation's products and services?

8. Which of these problems could you solve more successfully and what prevents you from doing this (internal bottleneck)?

9. Which problems do your target group perceive to be most pressing (survey results)?

10. How can you remain in contact with your target group (eg, customer seminars, workshops, advisory boards)?

42

What are the next steps to dealing with your target group's most pressing problem?

1. Note down all the problems of your target group that are in any way connected with your products or services

Limit yourself in this exercise to those problems that are within the broad scope of your field of business.

2. Rate your target group's problems according to their degree of urgency and put them in order of priority

Focus

Caution: The following selection and evaluation processes can only succeed if you are in continuing dialogue with your target group.

3. Evaluate your target group's pressing problems according to the following criteria:

Evaluation

- Which problem would your target group perceive as most pressing for them at the moment?
- Which of these problems could you with your current resources most convincingly and quickly in your target group's view?

Target group's pressing problems	*Subjective perception*	*Objective* competence*	Priority (A/B/C)

*'Objective' means that it is sufficient for the target group to believe that you are the best problem-solver. Whether this is objectively true makes no difference.

- Enter scores between 0 and 100. 100 points = highest score, ie, the problem perceived to be most pressing by the target group or the situation which you could solve most convincingly and quickly. It is also the case here that only practical tests will lead to the right outcome.

Your target group's most pressing problem (priority A) should henceforth be at the centre of your business. If you are not able to solve this problem convincingly in the near future, address yourself in the short term to another pressing problem (priority B), but continue to work on the solution to the most pressing problem.

4. My target group's most pressing problem is:

43

Summary: Seven principles for consistent focus on your target group

Stage 3: Most promising target group

1. Rethink: from a production focus to a target group focus.

2. Consider: target groups are people with the same problems or needs.

3. Concentrate on target groups and their particularly pressing problems.

4. Define your target group clearly, ie, as small and as homogeneous as possible.

5. Become the best and strongest problem-solver for your target group (= market leader).

6. Stay in constant touch with your target group (feedback as a learning process).

7. Constantly improve what you offer in consideration of the needs of your target group.

Implementation

Be sure to relate this stage fully to your own personal or business circumstances. Capture briefly your three most important thoughts or insights. 'Don't only th-ink it, ink it!' A catch phrase or a representative key word is sufficient.

My three most important thoughts, insights, key words:
-
-
-

Summary: Seven principles for permanent awareness of problems

Stage 4: Target group's most pressing problem

1. Think outwards rather than inwards: view everything through your target group's eyes.

2. Each target group has many different, distinctive problems.

3. Concentrate your activities on a target group's most pressing problem.

4. Enter into continuing dialogue with your target group about the most urgent problem.

5. The only decisive factor is which problem your target group perceives as most important to them.

6. Offer your target group some compelling benefits in the solution to their most pressing problem.

7. After solving the most pressing problem you must always address yourself to the next.

Be sure to relate this stage fully to your own personal or business circumstances. Capture briefly your three most important thoughts or insights. 'Don't only th-ink it, ink it!' A catch phrase or a representative key word is sufficient.

Implementation

> ## My three most important thoughts, insights, key words:
> -
> -
> -

45

Why is innovation your long-term strategic mission?

1. Your performance can and must always become better

Competition in many markets is so fierce today and the underlying conditions change so fast that standing still sooner or later restricts your ability to compete. Tom Peters, one of the world's most renowned business consultants, expresses this as 'innovate or die'.

2. The needs and problems of your customers change all the time

Since you want to be primarily the best problem-solver for your customers, you must also continually adjust what you offer those customers.

3. Innovation in the context of the EKS strategy means performance improvement

You will uncover a wide range of potential improvements – ranging from friendly behaviour to pioneering technical breakthroughs.

4. Using the EKS strategy significant innovations are possible even with limited resources

For further details see Stage 6, 'Cooperation strategy'.

5. Innovation must always focus on your target group's most pressing problem

Here, as a user of the EKS strategy, you are always a significant step ahead of the competition: your innovations are not indiscriminate and left more or less to chance, but are always firmly focused in each case on the target group's most pressing problem.

6. You reduce your investment risk to practically nil

The prerequisite is once again communication. Each step towards innovation must be directed by feedback from your target group.

How do you develop convincing innovations?

1. Define your target group's most pressing problem
Establish how your product or service must be designed in order to solve this problem in the best way or better than the competition.

'The best is the enemy of the good'

2. Look for opportunities for dialogue with your target group
Establish by talking to your target group whether your solution will be accepted. Then define the innovation as a preliminary concept on which you can concentrate all your efforts in future.

Dialogue with your target group

3. Analysis of internal bottlenecks: establish what prevents you from achieving that solution
Determine which internal bottlenecks you could remove with your own efforts and where you are lacking know-how and experience. Look for partners to collaborate with to overcome these obstacles (see Stage 6, 'Collaboration strategy').

Analysis of bottlenecks

4. Improve your information management
Focus on each obstacle and look in a targeted and systematic way for information that bridges the gap. Always record your work and set up a central point for collecting your ideas for innovations.

Information

5. Don't try to develop a solution to a problem that has already been solved by someone else
No problem is completely new – for many problems solutions have been developed in other areas or there are parallels in the natural world. Make it a principle to build on what other people have done, and start from there when developing your own solutions.

47

Which questions will enable you to make firm progress?

1. Which possibilities for fundamental improvements (innovations) do you see in your products and services?

2. Which innovations would solve the problem that the target group sees as most pressing?

3. Which members of the target group are suitable for an acceptability test?

4. What does the ideal solution to the problem look like?

5. How has the problem been solved up to now?

6. Which other possible solutions can you think of?

7. What prevents you from following the innovations through? Make a list of all conceivable obstacles!

8. Which obstacle hinders the innovation the most?

9. What information and expertise do you need to follow the innovation through?

10. Which bottlenecks could only be removed with the cooperation of a partner?

What are the next steps towards convincing innovation?

1. Starting with your target group's most pressing problem, formulate an ideal solution

Ideal solution

2. When you are certain that your solution is acceptable to the target group, divide the solution into its various stages and evaluate these according to your ability to complete them

Evaluation

Stages of performance improvement (innovation)	Score 0 50 100

Fill in scores between 0 and 100. Rough guidelines are:

100 points = highest score, ie, this stage can be completed with your own resources without external help (smallest obstacle);

50 points = can be completed with one-off or temporary help from outside;

0 points = only possible with the permanent collaboration of a partner (greatest obstacle).

3. Conduct the following check:

Check

4. Select the most suitable next step for innovation and write it here

5. My next step for innovation is:

49

Why do you need to cooperate to be successful?

'He who works alone, adds
– he who works with
others, multiplies'
(Oriental proverb)

1. To specialise you inevitably need to cooperate

Specialists are naturally dependent on working with other people. Since they only do themselves what they can do better than others, many tasks must be delegated. Working together can take quite different forms – from occasional, loose collaboration to a closer partnership.

2. Cooperation is always more successful than rivalry and competition

Competition is important as a driving force of progress in our performance-oriented society. That is accepted – but the fight for market share often costs money, resources and energy. It is much more sensible to stop this kind of waste and to combine resources in the interests of the customers.

3. Combining resources effectively increases your impact

First, collaboration frees up some resources that can be used for the benefit of your target group. Second, you can achieve the launch on to the market all the more quickly if you concentrate your efforts more precisely and strongly.

Synergy effect

4. Cooperation produces synergy

Partners can achieve more together than the sum of what each can produce alone – provided that they possess complementary capabilities. Partners with the same knowledge and capabilities cannot develop any synergies.

How do you find the best partner for cooperation?

1. Define the goal of the cooperation

In each case the goal should be jointly to increase the benefits to the target group. This is particularly important because the goal always lays down the route that the partnership will take. Only with this goal is lasting success assured.

'The ability to cooperate is the most important of all abilities in a network'

2. Always focus cooperation on obstacles

Expertise that is only required temporarily or on one occasion should always be acquired from external consultants.

Obstacles

3. Search systematically for partners to cooperate with

Don't leave the search to chance but consider as many people as possible who could help you to remove your bottlenecks (minimum group). Seek out a partner who possesses relevant expertise and with whom you have a good understanding.

Partners

4. Look for a complementary partner

Many people make the mistake of working with a partner who has the same knowledge and expertise. Such relationships make no sense because no synergies can develop.

Complementarity

5. Take care to reach agreement about the objectives of the cooperation

Be absolutely sure that you and your partner agree 100 per cent about your goals – or bring about such agreement if it is not present from the start. The objective of the cooperation must be its 'constitution'.

The same goals

6. Agree on an intellectual trial period

Before you invest even £1 together, agree on an intellectual trial period in which you can develop your first concept on a theoretical basis. Only if you can establish that you and your partner are 100 per cent in agreement should financial commitments be entered into.

Trial period

TO THE RESTAURANT

51

Which questions will enable you to make firm progress?

Write down the first words
and thoughts that come
into your head

1. Think back to Stage 5: what actual bottlenecks do you want to remove with the cooperation of a partner?

2. Which specialist capabilities and attributes should the partner contribute to remove these bottlenecks?

3. Which personal abilities and attributes should the partner contribute?

4. What do you expect your partner to do?

5. What can you offer your partner?

6. With what promises of success could you motivate your potential partner to collaborate with you?

7. In which way and using which media will you reach your minimum group (those people who could remove your bottleneck and who would be considered as partners for cooperation)?

8. Which synergies do you expect from the cooperation?

9. What is the common goal (the 'constitution' or 'basic law') of the cooperation?

10. How closely should you or do you want to work with your partner (loose arrangements, firm contracts and so on)?

52

What are the next steps towards optimal cooperation?

1. Define the common goal of your cooperation

We want to solve the most pressing problem

_____

of our most promising target group

_____

by offering the following (innovations):

• _____

• _____

• _____

2. List the obstacles to innovation and describe the desired attributes of your partner

Obstacles to innovation	Attributes of partner	Duration* (A/B/C)

*Note under 'duration' whether your partner will be needed always (A), occasionally (B) or only once (C).

3. Determine which groups of people meet the minimum criteria and make a motivating and potentially profitable proposal to them

4. Choose the partner with whom you have the greatest intellectual harmony

5. My optimal partner for cooperation could be:

Summary: Seven principles for successful innovation strategies

Stage 5: Innovation strategy

1. Always think innovatively: innovation means lasting performance improvement.

2. Your performance can and must be continually improving – standing still is a step backwards.

3. Your innovation must be directed at your target group's most pressing problem.

4. Collect all your ideas for innovation and evaluate them systematically.

5. Improve your information management and use your target group for evaluation.

6. Mobilise the potential ideas of colleagues and business partners.

7. Don't try to reinvent the wheel.

Implementation

Be sure to relate this stage fully to your own personal or business circumstances. Capture briefly your three most important thoughts or insights. 'Don't only th-ink it, ink it!' A catch phrase or a representative key word is sufficient.

My three most important thoughts, insights, key words:
-
-
-

54

Summary: Seven principles for successful cooperation strategies

Stage 6: Cooperation strategy

1. Think again: cooperation is always more successful than competition.

2. Strategically sound cooperation reduces competition to a minimum.

3. Always focus cooperation on bottlenecks – bring in external consultants from time to time.

4. Look for complementary partners for cooperation in order to develop common synergies.

5. Develop jointly some compelling benefits for a particular target group.

6. Be sure of 100 per cent agreement on the objectives of the cooperation.

7. Agree on an intellectual trial period before you make joint financial investments.

Be sure to relate this stage fully to your own personal or business circumstances. Capture briefly your three most important thoughts or insights. 'Don't only th-ink it, ink it!' A catch phrase or a representative key word is sufficient.

Implementation

My three most important thoughts, insights, key words:

-
-
-

55

Why is a constant basic need important to you?

'Having a target group is more important than having the means of production'

1. Specialising in variable needs is risky

Specialisation is dangerous if you concentrate on products or raw materials. These are 'variable', that is they can be altered or ultimately exchanged as required to fulfil certain needs or to solve problems.

Constant basic needs

2. Specialising in constant basic needs brings lasting success

Basic needs such as food, clothing, information, communication or mobility are constant. Almost everything which is used to satisfy these basic needs, including products, raw materials, know-how, management methods and so on is variable. Variables are continually being replaced by new solutions. Basic needs (ie, constants), in contrast, do not change.

For example, books and newspapers are encountering more and more competition from electronic media such as television, video, databases or multimedia. These products are all variable and satisfy the constant basic need for information.

Safeguarding your market

3. Safeguard your long-term market position

You should also safeguard your market position in the long term. Imitators throng on to the market sooner or later. Demand for any product or service is exhausted at some time. Products and services must therefore always be adapted to the changing problems and needs of the target group. Continual innovation which takes account of feedback from the target group is the basic prerequisite for long-term, risk-free specialisation and lasting success in the market.

How can you cover constant basic needs?

1. Set yourself the goal of becoming and remaining the best problem-solver for your target group

Define the constant basic need that is behind your target group's most pressing current problem.

The EKS strategy is a lifelong learning process. For the very reason that variables are constantly changing, performance must continually be improved through a double-loop learning process: you make your target group a proposal for improvement (feed-forward) and learn from their response (feed-back).

2. Make contact with your target group part of your normal operations

The double-loop learning process must take place on a continuing basis. Therefore try to establish a lasting exchange of information with representatives of your trusted and trustworthy clients through seminars or advisory boards.

3. Amass intangible rather than tangible assets

Tangible assets are worn out by use – in contrast, intangible assets like know-how, customer relationships and regular customers, patents and licences become more and more valuable through use. Material goods, not intangible assets, create dependence. Therefore you should always aspire to 'own' a target group rather than the means of production. You then function as a kind of broker between the target group, their search for a solution to their problems and what you are offering them, and all business comes through you.

4. Draw on, process, mass-produce your expertise

Even intangible assets can become tangible, for example in the form of software, a handbook, a checklist or an entire business concept (franchising). Mass produce your expertise with the help of partners and licensees, and use their experiences and feedback continually to improve your ideas. In short, turn yourself into a think tank which specialises in the problems of the target group. You can confidently leave the execution of your ideas to others.

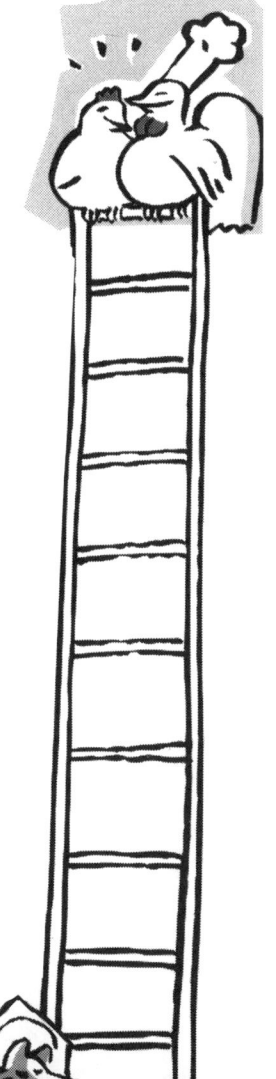

Which questions will enable you to make firm progress?

Write down the first words
and thoughts that come
into your head

1. Which continual basic need lies behind your target group's most pressing problem?

2. Which variable need will be met by what you offer, and which constant basic need lies behind it?

3. With which variable products and services can the constant basic need be covered?

4. Which ways exist now for you to satisfy the constant basic need of your target group?

5. How can you make long-term contact with your target group part of your normal operations?

6. Can your products and services take a form which is easy to mass produce?

7. Can you envisage offering your products and services as a franchise?

8. Which internal business functions could you potentially place outside, ie, could others undertake them for you? What could you completely or partly delegate to others?

9. Which business functions must you carry out yourself in all circumstances?

10. Can you envisage a circumstance which would jeopardise your long-term position in your field of business?

What are the next steps towards basic social needs?

1. Try to put into words the constant basic need that you are uncovering with the solution to your target group's most pressing problem. For example:

Constant basic need

- Not manufacturer of roof tiles, but solver of the problem of how to cover sloping roofs.
- Not seller of hamburgers, but provider of fast food for immediate consumption.
- Not organiser of time-management seminars, but solver of problems to do with time using different media (seminars, books, audio, video, computer software, multimedia, etc).

2. Complete the table with different ways of formulating the constant basic need, and evaluate them

Evaluation

Target group's constant basic needs	Priority* (A/B/C)

- Discuss the different possibilities with your partners and decide – analytically or intuitively – which seems the best alternative to you. *Rating: A = excellent, B = average, C = not so suitable.

3. Select the most appropriate formulation of your target group's most basic need
This must become your permanent mission or higher business goal. So, for example, every decision should be weighed against it to check whether it works towards the goal or not. This prevents you wasting your efforts.

4. The constant basic need of my target group is:

Summary: Seven principles for constant basic needs

Stage 7: Constant basic need

1. Your goal: become the 'owner' of target groups – instead of the 'owner' of the means of production.

2. Become and remain the best problem-solver and innovator for your target group.

3. Specialise in variable not constant basic needs.

4. Integrate the constant basic need into your business goals and mission.

5. Make contact with your target group part of your normal operations (double-loop learning process).

6. Make your intangible assets tangible by mass producing them.

7. Make yourself into a think tank and market your products and services through franchising.

Interpretation

Be sure to relate this stage fully to your own personal or business circumstances. Capture briefly your three most important thoughts or insights. 'Don't only th-ink it, ink it!' A catch phrase or a representative key word is sufficient.

My three most important thoughts, insights, key words:
-
-
-

60

Action plan: The step-by-step strategy for success

As Shakespeare said, 'suit the action to the word'. Studying this book will only have lasting benefits for you if you derive appropriate conclusions and action plans from it.

Review

What do you want to work on in detail and turn into firm action?							
Activity *on page*	Priority			Activities, tasks, next steps	Start: *planned for*	End: *finish by*	Check *complete? OK?*
	A	B	C				
26–29				Stage 1: Current situation and special strengths			
30–33				Stage 2: Most promising field of business			
36–39				Stage 3: Most promising target group			
40–43				Stage 4: Target group's most pressing problem			
46–49				Stage 5: Innovation strategy			
50–53				Stage 6: Cooperation strategy			
56–59				Stage 7: Constant basic need			

Case studies – typical applications of the EKS strategy

Now that you are aware of the four principles and seven stages of the EKS strategy, we would like to introduce you to three clear, practical examples of particularly successful applications of the strategy.

Since 1991 the Frankfurt-based accountancy firm KPMG Peat Marwick Treuhand GmbH and the FAZ Frankfurter Allgemeine Zeitung GmbH Information Service have given an annual management strategy prize for the 'best application of EKS'.

Three examples of successful strategy applications

Case study 1: Decorating firm – target-group-focused think tank at malerdeck, Germany

The first prize winner in 1991, Werner Deck, was distinguished above everyone else because of his ability to translate the business strategy of his decorating firm malerdeck GmbH into checklists and software which can easily be adapted by other businesses. His most important target group is now his licensees. He helps them to investigate their customers' most pressing problem, and advises them on their own management problems.

Draw on, process, mass produce

Case Study 2: Printing industry – model reorganisation at Gemini Graphics, India

One of the three EKS prize winners in 1992 was the Gemini printing company from India. The two people responsible for the reorganisation, Shenoy and Muthuswamy, were given the prize:

- first, because they achieved productivity improvements and specialisation in a distinctive way;
- second, because they demonstrated clearly that the EKS strategy leads to success even in a very unfavourable business environment.

Spirit more important than capital

Case Study 3: Appliance industry – consistent focus on a target group at Rational Catering Technology, Germany

Rational's success, likewise distinguished for various reasons, is based on an unusual business philosophy which has as its focus the needs and problems of customers. This organisation has risen to become world market leader with its managing partner Siegfried Meister at the helm. It realised how to market catering technology by focusing on service and the target group and to use this to create an innovative solution for cookery problems.

Customers at the centre

Case Study 1: Decorating firm – target-group-focused think tank at malerdeck, Germany

Learning points

This case documents the success story of a relatively simple distinction of target groups. To achieve this success it was necessary to alter the whole structure of the business and refocus the staff on to the most promising target group. Within the framework of the EKS strategy the learning processes necessary to achieve this kind of adjustment take a course which concentrates on obstacles and is therefore much faster – as a result of specialisation and focus.

EKS case study – decorating firm – malerdeck GmbH, Germany

- **Stage 1 – special strengths**: well organised, favourable location, staff and managers well motivated and flexible.

- **Stage 2 – most promising field of business**: painting work for private households.

- **Stage 3 – most promising target group**: prosperous, service-oriented people who are also prepared to pay for a specialist painter (pensioners with high incomes, well-paid employees as well as self-employed people and entrepreneurs).

- **Stage 4 – target group's most pressing problem**: jobs not being carried out on time, bad service, poor quality and no binding estimates of costs.

- **Stage 5 – innovations**: incorporating the staff, focusing the office workers on service, changing the way the operation is organised, communication strategy.

- **Stage 6 – partners for cooperation**: advertising agency, software developer, collaboration with other painting firms in the area and all over the country, joint purchasing with franchise partners.

- **Stage 7 – constant basic need**: the best problem-solver for private households, think tank for franchise partners, business advice for decorating firms, paint and varnish manufacturers.

Case history

When the young entrepreneur Werner Deck took over his parents' decorating firm of 50 employees in 1980, he inherited an absolute nightmare. Including accumulated interest, the bank overdraft stood at close to 1 million Deutsche Marks. The reason for this was frequent non-payment by customers. The Deck company worked mainly on new buildings for larger building firms and contractors, often for companies whose turnover was 1 million Deutsche Marks and more. That was a relatively large turnover for a decorating firm.

During the recession some customers went bankrupt or simply could not meet a considerable number of their bills. The Deck company and many other small firms were caught in this downward spiral. Because of poor liquidity the company accumulated, in addition to its bank overdraft, a tax debt to the revenue office of 350,000 Deutsche Marks. An audit would inevitably have led to the closure of all bank accounts and thus to bankruptcy. The business was barely keeping its head above water.

Werner Deck realised fairly rapidly that he would have to present the bank with a credible plan for rescuing the business quickly, in order to receive additional funds to settle the tax debt. In this situation he turned to the EKS strategy.

EKS Stage 1: Analysis of the current situation

The analysis of the current situation revealed that about 90 per cent of the firm's turnover came from new building and rebuilding work. In this market there was relentless competition based on price. The profit margin was at most between 3 and 5 per cent, on large contracts sometimes even nil.

The risk of receiving no money or only part payment from unreliable building contractors was extremely high. Because of the pressure on prices work had to be done very quickly and at considerable loss of quality. That led to defects which entailed further costs in putting them right. In addition the building trade always experiences gaps in new building work in the winter.

EKS Stage 2: Most promising field of business

Since Werner Deck did not want to expose himself to this repressive competition any further, he looked for another field of business and more promising target groups. When he analysed in more detail the customers who made up the remaining small part of the company's turnover, namely the private customers, he discovered the following:

- Private customers were usually happy with the painters, when they arrived.
- Price did not play a decisive role. Although the total contract price was only between DM500 and 2000, the profit margin was between 10 and 20 per cent.
- All invoices were paid more or less on time, and there was practically no risk of private customers failing to pay.
- Because of the lack of pressure on prices it was possible to carry out defect-free, quality work.
- Seasonal fluctuations did not apply since work could be carried out indoors all year round.

Building crisis

Imminent bankruptcy

Reorganisation plan

1. Analysis of current situation

Strong price competition

Low profit margins

2. Field of business

Private customers

Small private contracts nevertheless have an annoying disadvantage: the amount of organisational time required to calculate and quote for the job is almost as much as that for a large contract. For this reason the target group of private customers had been neglected until now. The analysis further revealed that almost all competitors had done the same. Instead of labour-intensive 'trifles' they preferred the apparently lucrative large contracts. Only small firms with up to five employees were active in this field of business.

3. Target groups

EKS Stage 3: Most promising target group

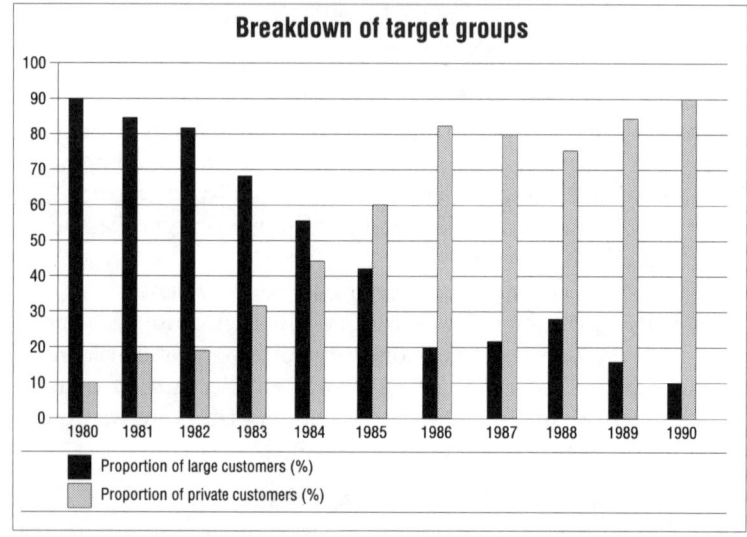

All the firm's energy and resources were immediately concentrated on private customers and their problems, but without neglecting the previous target groups for the time being. Deck split the 'private customer' target group even further into three sub-groups: one-third did the work themselves, another third used 'moonlighters', the rest commissioned a specialist firm. Deck drew from this remaining third two promising target groups:

Well paid

• Well paid academics, self-employed people and entrepreneurs who did not have time or did not want to do the work themselves and were looking for a complete solution to their problem.

Older

• Older private customers, who could no longer do the work themselves, but who possessed enough money to be able to commission a firm with a full range of services.

Further differentiation
of target groups

66

EKS Stage 4: Target group's most pressing problem

In the multitude of unsolved problems lay the key to success:

- The target group complained that trades people are so hard to find.
- Trades people are – if they actually arrive – almost always unpunctual.
- Painters as a rule leave behind dirt and mess.
- Clearing furniture to allow painting work to be carried out is often left to the customer.
- Competent advice on choice of colours and wallpaper is not very often available.

Werner Deck wanted to concentrate on a faultless service and the private customer's minimum factor: quality work together with punctuality, friendliness, guaranteed prices, cleanliness and competent advice.

With this strategy as 'security' Werner Deck was able to inspire confidence at the bank. He received not only the DM350,000 urgently required for the revenue office, but also additional funds to put the strategy into practice. Deck informed the revenue office and bankruptcy was averted. In this case you can clearly see the persuasive power of intangible assets such as a good strategy.

Bank loan

The power of intangible assets

EKS Stage 5: Innovation strategy

Now it was a question of turning the idea into reality. As normal for a new strategic direction, the obstacles (internal minimum factors) have to be removed by focusing resources on them.

5. Innovation

First obstacle: degree of awareness

Awareness of the company among private customers was almost nil. This obstacle was removed with the help of an advertising agency. For the new company name, 'malerdeck', a multi-coloured logo was developed. This corporate identity was designed to be used in publicity material: on letter headings, in advertisements, on scaffolding, on company vehicles. The advertisements first acted as image building and later addressed the target group's most pressing problem: 'Do your painters leave dirt and mess? We don't. Give us a call! We will prove it to you.' In 1987 Werner Deck received the 'German trade prize' from the business magazine *Impulse* for this corporate identity.

New corporate identity

Next the contracting process had to be radically speeded up. At the latest two days after a client has telephoned a malerdeck employee arrives to establish what is required. This person considers the customer's problems exclusively. He will discuss alternatives, give preliminary design suggestions and agree on a binding timetable – if necessary including Saturdays, Sundays or evenings. All work to be done will be described and contained in a precise, written quotation.

The calculation of quotations and invoicing still took too long. Therefore a computer was invested in and special software developed. Now the quotation could be with the customer as early as two days later – with a fixed-price guarantee. The customer was thus safe from unpleasant surprises. While competitors were still calculating the quotation, the staff from malerdeck had often already begun the work. This software has become the leading trade programme and in 1989 it received the 'German software prize' from the business magazine *Impulse*.

Speed and service are today part of every stage of the contract. Malerdeck also handles even the smallest jobs which no other painter would take on.

EKS Stage 6: Cooperation

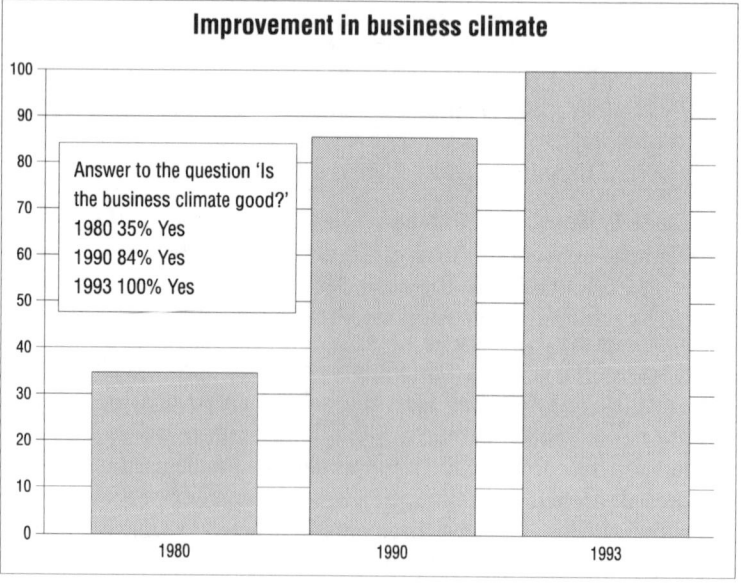

Improvement in business climate

Answer to the question 'Is the business climate good?'
1980 35% Yes
1990 84% Yes
1993 100% Yes

If the customer decides to place an order, as a rule the work has to be carried out very quickly. With the help of precise scheduling malerdeck can almost always accommodate the customer's wishes – with the help of its partners. To be able to react quickly to customers' requests every time, Deck collaborates with ten other small businesses, which have between two and eight employees.

Case Study 1

Dealing with bottlenecks through other small businesses

The precise time that the work will begin and the agreed timetable will be confirmed to the customer, together with the guaranteed fixed price. Of course, the painters arrive at the agreed time. They are friendly and competent, they move around the customer's house very carefully and carry out good quality work. At the end of the job everything is cleaned and vacuumed. Together with the customer the result is examined and the customer's opinion recorded. Mistakes and defects are rectified immediately.

Fixed-price guarantee

In retrospect Deck claims that staff motivation was the most difficult element of the new direction. On large building sites good manners are not required, nor is there a marked service mentality. These very qualities, however, form the foundation of Deck's new business concept. This obstacle was removed at first with the help of external trainers. Today Werner Deck takes on the task.

Third obstacle: staff

Malerdeck's whole business concept was recorded in checklists. Therefore Deck could engage three additional employees to manage the business and now has more time to concern himself with his target group's problems. The entire 'malerdeck' concept (including checklists, corporate identity, the whole method of organisation) has been marketed since 1986 in a system similar to franchising. A new logo was created for this – 'Opti-Maler-Partner'. Up to 1993, 66 businesses were already working successfully in this way, including three in Austria, and together they are achieving a turnover of about DM115 million. A licence to cover a particular region costs DM12,000 and the annual fee is DM1000. Deck advises the partner businesses about anything from office organisation, through marketing and advertising to time management. Twice a year Deck invites his partners to a two-day management conference. The focal point is transferring know-how about management information and methods.

Productivity improvements through checklists

Cooperation with franchise partners

Werner Deck wants to take this cooperation still further in the future, so he will be active in improving the logistics of the partner firms. The partners no longer have to worry about quotations, invoicing, purchasing materials or calculations and they can already buy their materials from Deck's wholesalers on particularly good terms.

Purchasing cooperation

EKS Stage 7: From production-oriented to innovation-oriented business

For some years Werner Deck has been active as a business adviser. He advises trade colleagues primarily, but also wholesalers and paint and varnish manufacturers. Among others he trains salespeople from various industries in sales techniques. Three of the largest paint manufacturers wanted to sign an exclusive supply contract with Deck. He decided on the European market leader, thereby taking the step from being a production-oriented to an innovation-oriented business. Deck took over the function of being a 'target-group-focused think tank' for his partner businesses in the future. His chief task today consists in exploring his target group's problems still more thoroughly and developing still more perfect solutions. In future what he offers will be aligned even more strongly with the most promising target group, the wealthy group of house owners, self-employed people and those of independent means.

Outcome

The proportion of private customers has continued to increase from year to year. In 1990 the ratio of large customers to private customers was almost the reverse of that in 1980. Now only 10 per cent falls in the unprofitable property area, the rest in the desired target group.

Since 1993 a new target group has been cultivated – the demanding highest earners. Under malerdeck's leadership in collaboration with an interior decorator and a furnishing expert, rooms, apartments or whole houses can be creatively decorated with exclusive and individual painting techniques and at the same time refurnished. This service already accounts for 20 per cent of turnover.

The financial situation has also improved. The bank was ready to invest further in the firm. Between 1980 and 1987, the DM1 million overdraft was paid off with the interest. In 1991 a new office building was purchased for DM1.8 million, a third of which was paid in cash.

To supplement his offering Werner Deck founded the firm 'bodendeck' with his brother. This concentrates entirely on floor coverings for private customers – offering the same service as at malerdeck. In 1980 only 35 per cent of employees judged the business climate to be good, but in 1990 it was already 84 per cent and in 1993 as high as 100 per cent (see graph on page 68). The customers are also very satisfied. Deck says: 'The relationship with our customers can be described as "friendship".'

Even if you do not possess either a distinctive competence or better problem-solving experience than your competitors, with the right strategy, namely focusing resources on the most pressing problem of a tightly defined target group, you can quickly become number one – entirely in accordance with the perception that in the country of the blind the one-eyed man is king.

Success through the right strategy

Case study 2: Printing industry – model reorganisation at Gemini Graphics, India

Through strategy successfully out of bankruptcy

Learning points

The case of the Indian printing firm Gemini Graphics shows how with the right strategy an almost bankrupt business can be rescued step by step without an injection of capital.

EKS case study – printing industry – Gemini Graphics, India

- **Stage 1 – special strengths**: regularly recurring printing contracts with large runs including consecutive numbering.

- **Stage 2 – most promising field of business**: lottery tickets, cheques, share certificates.

- **Stage 3 – most promising target group**: lottery companies, public customers.

- **Stage 4 – target group's most pressing problem**: punctual, reliable delivery of lottery tickets.

- **Stage 5 – innovation**: defect-free stamping with on-line numbering at high speed.

- **Stage 6 – partners for cooperation**: employees (internal) and competitors (external).

- **Stage 7 – constant basic need**: specialist in authenticated copies of high-value official certificates.

Case history

About 120 km south of Hyderabad in southern India lies Bidar. There in 1989 the printing firm Gemini Graphics Private Limited was as good as bankrupt. Yet G G Shenoy, one of the managers, had done everything imaginable to satisfy his customers. Gemini took on any order that was technically challenging and still managed to achieve very good quality. The firm was supported by an extremely active salesforce with sales offices or agents in the large cities of Bombay, Madras, Hyderabad, Bangalore and Calcutta. The marketing department carried out market research, implemented every normal sales and administrative activity, and conducted detailed investigations if an order fell through the net.

Wasted resources

Current situation

Still the company was practically bankrupt. Losses totalled 10 million rupees. The main bank cancelled all lines of credit. The remaining banks threatened to shut the firm down until their debts were paid.

Gemini's auditors likewise suggested that Shenoy should close the firm and announce bankruptcy. The suppliers also did not want to sell Gemini anything more because of the threatened bankruptcy and the enormous outstanding debts. Exceptions were only made if payment was received in advance. Since the employees' salaries could no longer be paid on time, their motivation also began to dwindle.

The firm's central bottleneck

On account of the hopeless losses and in spite of a cushion of six months' orders, a desperate situation was reached. The marketing department and the previous management had always seen the cause of the problem as insufficient sales. Therefore on Gemini's off-set litho machine everything was printed that the marketing department could attract from all over the country: computer forms, company annual reports, textbooks, prospectuses, calendars and much more. Because of the constant retooling and the related machine down-time, a reasonable profit could never be achieved with the exceedingly low prices at which they were operating. Higher prices could not be charged, however, owing to the competitive situation at the time.

Using the EKS strategy

When the organisation was right at the end of the line, Shenoy took over sole management. Through studying the EKS distance-learning course via the Indian Baroda Productivity Council, it became clear to him that against all expectations his organisation's obstacle did not lie in a lack of orders at all, but in the fact that the wrong orders were continually being taken on. The more orders arrived, the larger the losses became. This was thus the central obstacle and also the most effective starting point for the strategy. The solution could therefore only be found by identifying and obtaining the 'right' orders.

Shenoy was still sceptical at the beginning about the EKS strategy. He consulted the director of the Baroda Productivity Council, Narayan Muthuswamy, about which steps he should take.

EKS Stage 1: Analysis of special strengths

They began immediately with the strengths analysis and analysed Gemini's few special successes. A few particularly profitable projects were included, but also those successes which had been particularly praised by the customers. Muthuswamy did not only talk to Gemini's management but also to the most important customers, the suppliers and the banks.

The analysis brought the following strengths to light:

1. Technical competence in high-quality colour printing.

2. Trust in the integrity of Shenoy, the manager.

3. Employees who endeavoured to achieve punctual delivery, provided that paper and other materials were actually in stock.

4. The printing machinery – in this case a Canadian offset litho machine which could run at high speed (up to 400 m per minute) and was therefore predominantly intended for large orders.

5. Gemini possessed a system which allowed consecutive numbering of printed material.

6. The printing company could dispatch completed orders to several addresses.

Special strengths

Up to now the organisation's special strengths had been completely neglected, ie, regularly recurring printing contracts with large runs including consecutive numbering, which had to be sent to different locations. Previously the firm had handled small runs which could be produced as well or better by a thousand other printing companies with less sophisticated technology.

2. Fields of business

EKS Stage 2: Most promising field of business
The second step was to look for the kind of work which would theoretically be best suited to these strengths.

Listing

a) Listing as many fields of business as possible
A brainstorming session produced the following printed objects:

1. Securities, bonds, company share certificates, national savings certificates.

2. Development certificates for the states of Maharashta, Madras and Kerala. The related inspection documents and reply coupons only had to be printed when the machine had free capacity.

3. Bills of exchange, cheques and travellers cheques.

4. Lottery tickets for south Indian states.

5. Bottle labels for Hyderabad and Karnataka.

6. Gift vouchers.

7. Order forms for letters of credit from various banks.

8. Labels for the Export Inspection Agency in Bombay, Madras and Calcutta.

9. Ballot papers for various states and the Election Committee in New Delhi.

b) Evaluation of fields of business

The next step was to choose from this list five types of order which were in constant demand and five with long print runs.

Since the economic situation was already very difficult, in each case the job with the highest ratio of profit contribution to time spent was determined. After applying the selection principle 'better unique than interchangeable', three types of order remained: lottery tickets, cheques and share certificates.

Lottery tickets were chosen because:

1. Gemini was located in the region where 60 per cent of all India's lottery tickets were purchased. The ticket printers were nevertheless situated without exception in northern India;

2. the demand for tickets was greater than the supply;

3. absolutely no mistakes in numbering were permitted; and

4. the tickets had to be distributed to different sales points.

In favour of cheques were the increasing demand for them, the requirement for high quality and the fact that Shenoy was one of the few experts in the country who possessed the know-how to produce this kind of document. Nevertheless many other printers had already discovered this field of business.

Printing share certificates was interesting for Gemini because eight different processes were necessary to guarantee against forgery. Gemini's machine could perform all eight in one operation. In addition, quick colour changes were required (which no other printer could do), as well as continuous numbering and delivery to different locations. By chance a new issue was then due for India's largest corporation, and also by chance Gemini had previously handled a similar order for the same customer who had been completely satisfied.

Evaluation

Lottery tickets

Cheques

Share certificates

75

Initially the third option, printing share certificates, was adopted in order to bridge the financial gap until the first order for lottery tickets could be obtained.

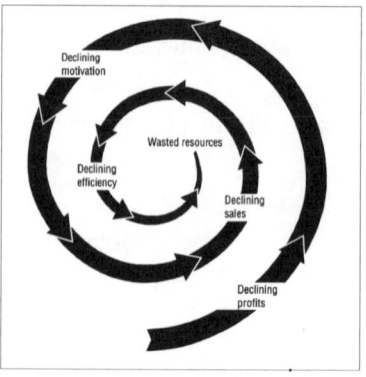

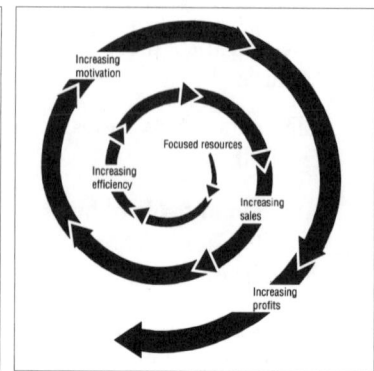

The spiral of failure   The spiral of success

3. Target group

EKS Stage 3: Most promising target group

Contact with target group

Shenoy succeeded against stiff competition in obtaining the contract to print 90 per cent of the largest issue of shares in India. The order was also obtained completely according to the principles of EKS. During the discussions the customer was asked specifically about his problems, while competitors restricted themselves to

Ask about problems

questions about the contractual requirements. In the event there were plenty of problems. Indian law prescribes, for example, that every share certificate must be signed by hand. Since the market value of each share certificate is only pence, the costly manufacturing process required was extremely unprofitable. Shenoy could offer

Offer a solution

a solution for this problem by using a machine which reproduced a signature automatically. These and similar solutions to problems meant that the contract was given to Gemini. The customer was even able to be persuaded to finance and deliver the necessary paper and other materials. In this way the largest obstacle, namely the lack of materials because of the company's financial situation, was overcome, at least in this case. Within a month a net profit was achieved, and with this as support the first contract for lottery tickets was tendered for.

4. Target group's problems

EKS Stage 4: Target group's most pressing problem

After three months of concentrated effort the first order for lottery tickets was finally obtained. Since then the business has not taken on any other type of order and has remained unconditionally loyal

Punctual delivery

to its target group. The new venture succeeded because the firm focused on its target group's most pressing problem: punctual delivery of lottery tickets. The 'shelf-life' of a ticket is only 15 days after printing. Each day's delay in delivery means a reduction in sales of 6.5 per cent. The printers far away in northern India could never completely eliminate the risk of delay, and their numbering was likewise not completely reliable.

Gemini managed to become the best problem solver in its market:

Target group's best problem-solver

- It guarantees absolutely faultless numbering, since it would be disastrous if two winners with the same ticket number were to dispute the first prize.
- Paper and printing are of very high quality, because the image of the lottery company depends largely on the appearance of its tickets.

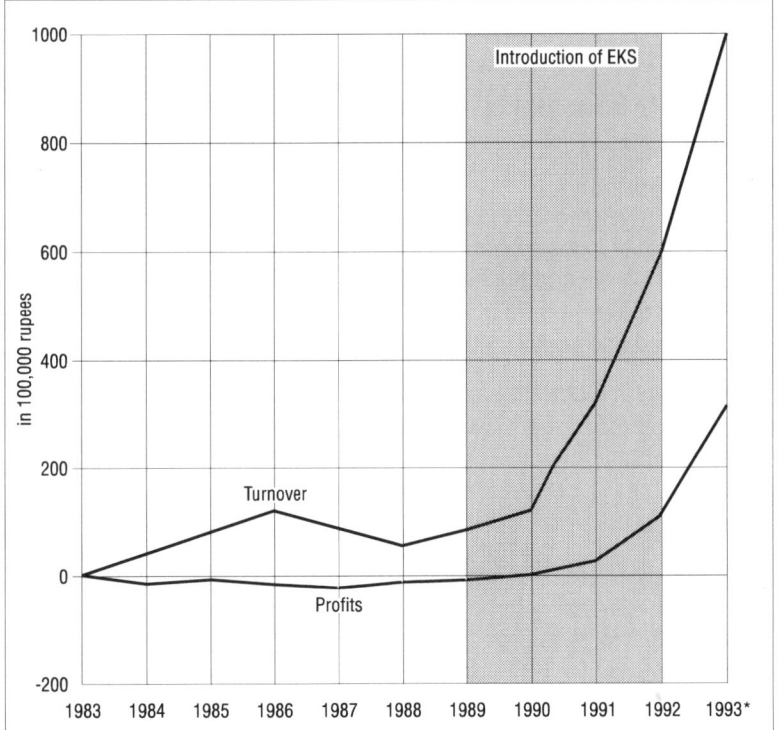

Gemini Graphics' profit and turnover   *1993 value estimated based on half-year results
Source: Gemini Graphics Public Limited

Gemini made available to its customers rooms where they could sort and despatch the tickets themselves. In addition it helped the customers with the design of new games. After solving the technical and logistical problems (quality of tickets), Gemini thus addressed the target group's next problem.

Most recent example: since time and again there is friction between the revenue office and the lottery companies about the tax to be paid, Gemini is now looking for a solution to this problem as well.

5. Innovation

EKS Stage 5: Innovation strategy

Shenoy and Muthuswamy developed innovations on both technical and organisational levels. These included the prevention of errors by on-line numbering. On every ticket a number must be stamped three times. Due to the enormous speed of the process the stamping operation must work smoothly. This problem was solved on the technical level. In countless other small ways everything was done to achieve a trouble-free operation and optimal use of capacity.

Through specialisation productivity increased thirteen-fold from 15,000 to 200,000 items per day. Before long it should have reached 300,000 per day.

6. Cooperation

EKS Stage 6: Cooperation strategy

- *Internal cooperation*: all employees are familiar with the strategy. Promotion and salary increases are related to performance (principle of internal customers).
- *External cooperation*: printing orders that do not fit into Gemini's field of business are passed on to other printers. By the same token Gemini also receives orders via previous competitors. Instead of competing they now collaborate.

7. Constant basic need

EKS Stage 7: Constant basic need

Best problem-solver

Shenoy and his staff have succeeded in defining themselves as the best problem-solver for punctual and reliable printing of lottery tickets, share certificates and other authenticated, individually numbered documents in large quantities.

Positive growth spiral

Gemini operates 24 hours a day, seven days a week, and this is currently the largest internal bottleneck. The business is in a positive growth spiral. It paid off the losses of the previous seven years within two years. In 1989, when Shenoy first heard of EKS, Gemini made a loss of 1.4 million rupees. In 1991 its profits were 2.4 million rupees, in 1992 10.4 million. Turnover over the same period

Material success

rose from 11.2 (1989) to 60 million (1992). In 1993 turnover reached about 100 million rupees, and profits also increased.

The two people responsible for the reorganisation, Shenoy and Muthuswamy, see their biggest success in the fact that they brought back to life a business which had been declared completely dead – and this without the injection of any capital.

Case Study 3: Appliance industry – consistent focus on a target group at Rational Catering Technology, Germany

Learning points

This case shows how you can compensate for numerous weaknesses – which every person and every business has – by total concentration on a few strengths. It is a question essentially of focusing on the obstacle to your own development and that of your customers.

EKS case study – appliance industry – Rational Catering Technology GmbH, Germany

- **Stage 1 – special strengths**: technical know-how in production of metal goods (including ovens).

- **Stage 2 – most promising field of business**: ovens for the catering industry.

- **Stage 3 – most promising target group**: professional caterers.

- **Stage 4 – target group's most pressing problem**: lack of space, combination ovens (simultaneous steam and convection heat), energy efficient and time-saving ovens.

- **Stage 5 – innovation strategy**: parallel combination ovens taking up a small amount of space.

- **Stage 6 – cooperation strategy**: continual dialogue directly with the target group.

- **Stage 7 – constant basic need**: specialist in catering ovens.

Case history

Rational Catering Technology GmbH, located in Landsberg am Lech about 100 km from Munich, was originally a supplier of high-grade steel goods. Many target groups were accordingly served by its very wide range.

When founding partner Siegfried Meister took over management of the company in 1976, convection (high pressure – dry air) ovens began to be manufactured for the first time. These were installed in large kitchens to cook with hot air, ie, dry heat. Rational was a pioneer in this area.

79

Since Meister was convinced that the business needed to stand on more than one leg to lessen the risk, further diversification was energetically pursued – including sauna ovens. At that time turnover was about 2.88 million Deutsche Marks, and after all kinds of effort in technology and marketing the following year it rose a meagre DM20,000 to 2.9 million. Since profits did not rise, price increases were necessary for the hot-air ovens. However, this meant that demand decreased and turnover continued to stagnate. The more the company tried to solve its problems with individual measures, first without and then with advisers, the more individual problems were discovered: with bookkeeping, production, premises, marketing. Doubt gradually grew about this method. In 1978 turnover was only DM3.18 million and neither in 1979 was any improvement shown. Slowly Meister came to suspect that the entire method and way of thinking was wrong – ie, dissecting problems to turn the price screw and extract the last penny from the customer.

The turning-point

In September 1980 Meister came across the EKS strategy and realised quickly that it was describing *his* problem exactly. A business needs a clear basic mission in order to offer benefits. True benefits can only be offered to a clearly defined target group. Meister was pleased that in the first place he had to look for and build on his strengths, since previously he had mainly looked for weaknesses – and ultimately also found them.

The conclusive break with his former thinking came when the sales manager came back from a trade fair with some bad news. No fewer than 34 manufacturers had exhibited hot-air ovens at the fair. This pointed to a price war in the future.

Meister kept entirely to the EKS philosophy: 'competition yes, repressive competition, no'. For him that meant using innovation to offer his target group distinctly better benefits than his competitors, instead of taking part in a general price war in the market for standard products.

A new solution

Meister developed a new product for his target group, professional chefs in large kitchens, and eventually brought to the market a revolutionary new development – the combination steam oven. With this appliance it became possible for the first time to cook as one chose using a steam generator with damp or dry heat separately, successively or in combination. The particular innovation was in the electrical controls, which allowed the steam to be operated com-

Price increases

Declining turnover

Basic social mission = offer benefits

34 competitors

No price competition

New development for the target group

pletely separately. By this means 70 or 80 per cent of all cooking processes in a large kitchen could be handled in a single appliance – taking up only a square metre of space. This had three immediate advantages for the target group: rationalisation of cooking processes, better working conditions and better quality food.

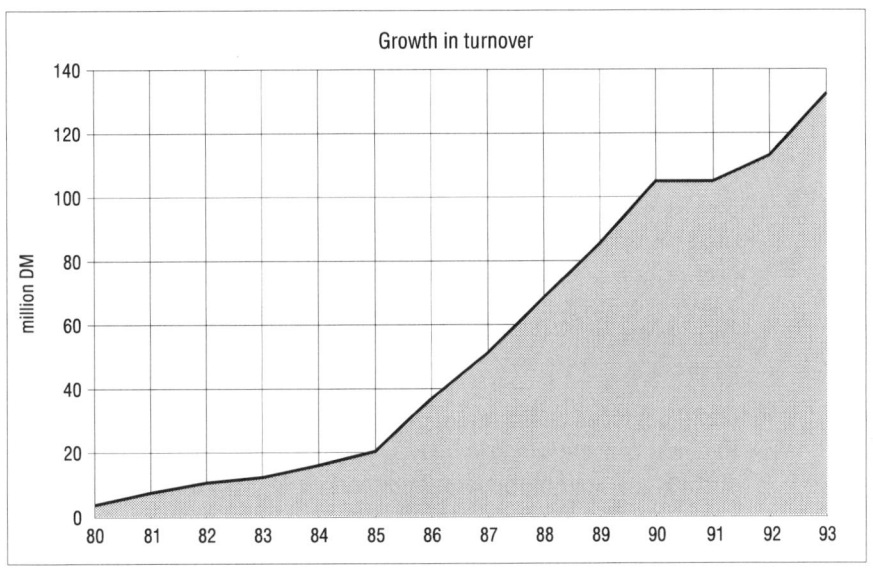

Growth in turnover

Meister now faced the problem of bringing the new product to the market with the limited resources of a medium-sized business. About 70 per cent of the firm's capacity was tied up in producing hot-air ovens. Against the opposition of his staff, Meister took a large risk: he stopped offering the previous oven overnight and concentrated exclusively on the combination steam oven. Meister was convinced that he could only reach a dominant market position by doing this. Nevertheless you should be warned against doing the same – copying this strategy is only to be recommended when you are completely sure of your ground. Normally in this kind of situation it would be better to let the old product run alongside the new one without expending any further effort on the former and cut back gradually on the numbers supplied. The EKS strategy does not teach you to jump from one field of business to another, but to walk carefully.

Total concentration on a solution to the problem = combination steam oven

EKS: don't jump, walk instead

However, the commercial success proved Meister right. Turnover rose from DM3.91 million in 1980 through 8.6 million in 1983 to 104 million in 1990. In 1993 it was about 135 million. Of course it was also hard earned. Nevertheless, if the profit exceeds a set rate

Commercial success

prices will fall, because ultimately the company does not want to exploit the target group.

The competition

Rational was once again worldwide pioneer in its market and this automatically attracted competitors. Rational's patent was circumvented by small modifications. The other suppliers, it is true, were not in a position to copy Rational's strategy: they still worked according to the old recipe, ie, price competition as a first move. Rational behaved differently. Through concentrating on a single product in growing numbers, Rational can naturally benefit from the advantages of specialisation such as lower costs. But that on its own is not sufficient. Besides, mere price competition would not meet the goal of the EKS strategy. If you enter into competition over prices, in the long run your profits will be nil. Rational secured a lead over the competition above all through its very close contact with its target group and continual innovation and improvement of its product.

Continual focus on the target group

Rational concentrated exclusively on its target group of 'professional chefs'. All staff in the sales and marketing departments worked for a set time in a kitchen learning how everything related together, to be able to deal with the customer's day-to-day problems directly. All 450 employees think only about combination ovens day after day and about how they can make the daily work of professional cooks all over the world easier and achieve the best performance.

At Rational 14 chefs are responsible for maintaining close, personal contact with the target group all over the world. They are both 'advocates' for the target group at Rational and transmitters of the Rational message in the customers' language. The chefs have an important say at Rational – extending as far as the development department. They are often on the road, briefing other chefs about Rational products and listening a great deal to what the customers are saying. The chefs speak the customers' language.

In addition, Rational has the use of a very modern training centre. There free seminars can be organised for the target group. This contact intensifies the links with the target group.

Personnel policy

Such peak performance can, of course, only be achieved with highly motivated employees. Staff motivation is high on Rational's list of priorities, in accordance with the focus on the target group. Each employee is ultimately there to offer the target group the best possible benefits. This is the central ingredient of the common business philosophy. So lying to or cheating customers is forbidden, and the penalty is dismissal.

The Rational business philosophy

Based on the EKS strategy, all staff work according to the following principles:

- All resources are used to offer the best possible benefits to a clearly defined target group, instead of pursuing profit maximisation as the highest goal.

- Focus and specialisation on one of the target group's fundamental, central problems instead of wasting resources through diversification.

- Well motivated, self-reliant employees from the top to the bottom of the organisation, instead of a hierarchy mentality.

- Well informed closeness to the customer as the supreme goal for all employees.

Outcome

Turnover distribution 1993

Inland 40%

Export 60%

Market leader

Prize winner

The outcome of this strategy can be clearly seen. Rational is the market leader in combination steam ovens with a worldwide market share of about 50 per cent. Rational is represented in all industrialised countries, and in addition combination ovens are manufactured under licence in several countries and there are distribution partners in 45 countries. In 1993, 60 per cent of turnover came from overseas. Because of the larger volume of sales turnover per employee rose from DM85,000 in 1980 to DM340,000 – a clear effect of specialisation. The business has won countless honours and prizes, for example the 'Federal Innovation Prize' in 1991 from the Trade and Industry Minister and the 'Award for Distinguished Development' from the Food Service Consultants Society International, as well as the 'Hamburg Prize – Food Service 1989' from a German technical publisher.

Dangerous specialisation?

Specialisation on the solution to a problem

Now as then, within the industry Meister's strategy of specialisation is still considered to be very dangerous, despite its impressive success. Meister is not affected by such objections: 'We are not specialists in combination steam ovens, but in modern ovens. We are not only specialists in a single product with different variations and models, but we offer in each case the *best* solution to the problem. Each of the 450 employees thinks about solving cooking problems – particularly the 30 development engineers. That ensures that we remain market leaders in innovation. We are offering the combination steam oven today not by chance, because nothing else occurred to us in the area of catering ovens – but because *for the time being* it is the best solution to the problem.

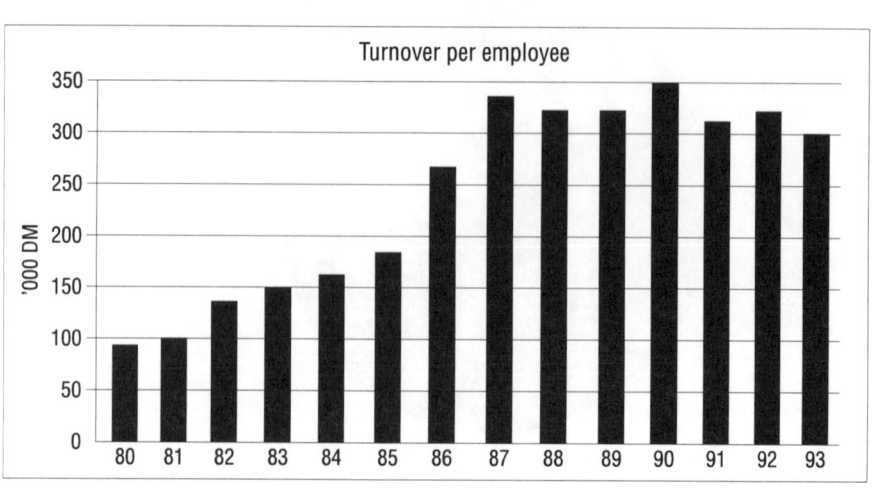

Index